GODS OF INDIA

Ganesha Wins the Race

SHUBHA VILAS

Ganesha, was created by Parvati from turmeric paste and soon became her beloved son. Lord Shiva also doted on him. He is the most adorable of gods with a lovable face and a round stomach. Ganesha is also worshipped as the god of intelligence and wisdom.

Lord Ganesha's name is taken before any auspicious occasion in every Hindu household despite the presence of 36 crore deities. But how did he gain that position?

Once, Lord Shiva announced a competition for all the gods and goddesses. His thundering voice boomed across the heavenly horizon informing the participants that they had to circle the whole world thrice on their respective vehicles. The winner of the competition would forever be the first and foremost to be worshipped in all the worlds and would help overcome obstacles.

All the deities gathered for the event. Indra came on his mighty elephant. Durga on her ferocious lion. Yamaraj sported his buffalo and Saraswati her swan. A murmur of dissent went up in the air when Aditya arrived on seven horses and Vayu on his thousand horses!

Lord Ganesha was feeling depressed as the test was to complete the Parikrama of the whole Universe. His vehicle was a mouse. To expect a mouse to surpass the other swifter vehicles of the other deities was absurd. All the others had a good laugh when they saw Ganesha.

Why had Ganesha chosen the mouse as his vehicle? It had so happened that once Krauncha, a celestial musician god, accidentally stepped on Muni Vamadeva's foot, who got enraged and cursed him to become a mouse. Once, the mouse was trying to destroy Maharshi Parashar's ashram.

Lord Ganesha who was present there, looped his noose around the mouse and said, 'Krauncha...you have caused a lot of trouble but I pardon you and shall use you as my vehicle.'

The mouse can slither through tiny holes and narrow pathways, and carry Lord Ganesha to the nooks and corners of the world to destroy obstacles.

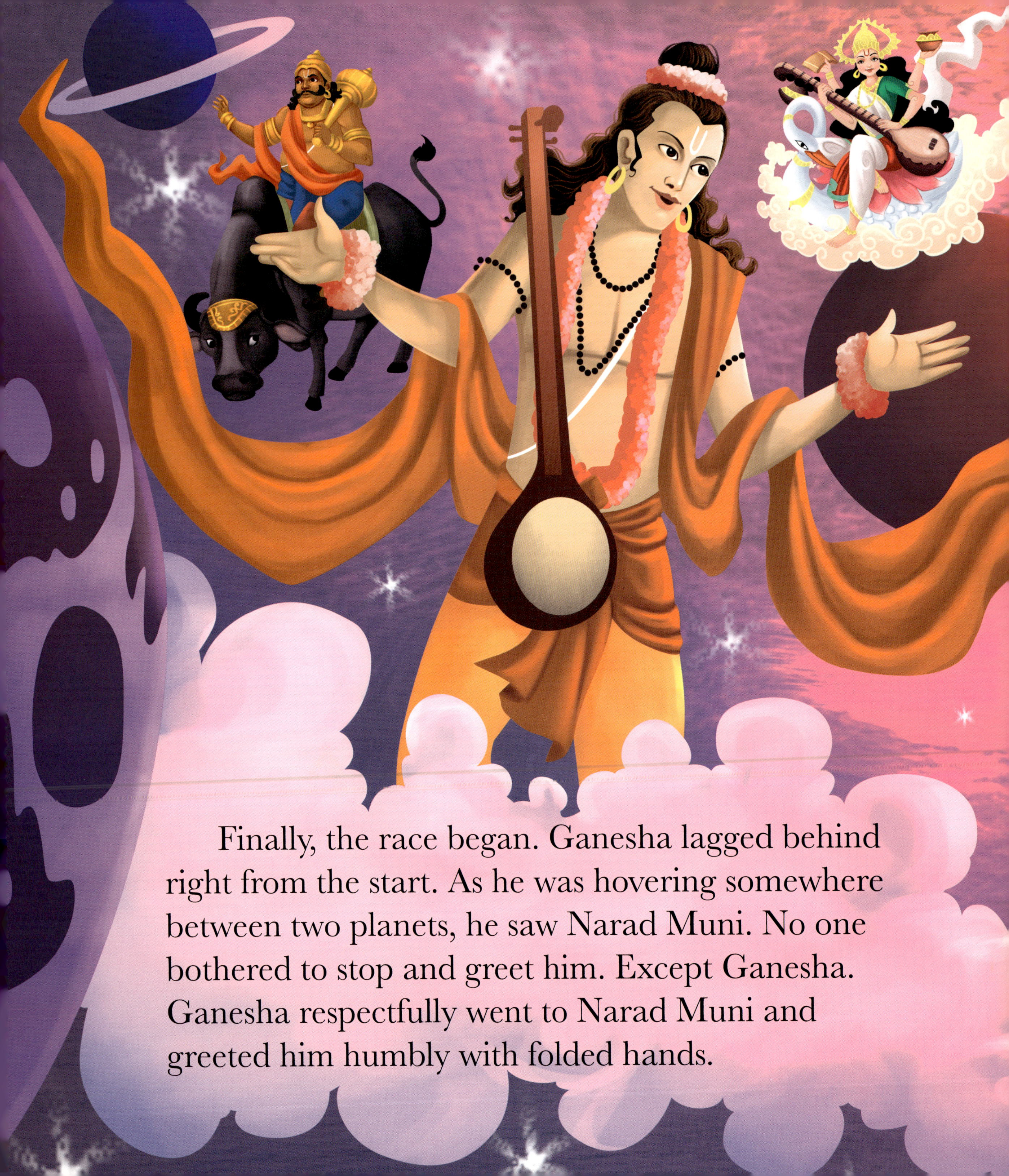

Finally, the race began. Ganesha lagged behind right from the start. As he was hovering somewhere between two planets, he saw Narad Muni. No one bothered to stop and greet him. Except Ganesha. Ganesha respectfully went to Narad Muni and greeted him humbly with folded hands.

'My dear Ganesha!' Narada exclaimed with joy. 'What is going on? Where are all these exalted gods rushing to?' enquired the sage.

When he heard about the competition, Narada understood now why all the gods were running. No one wanted to stop and greet him lest they got delayed. They even avoided looking at him.

Narada Muni was touched that Ganesha was the only one who actually stopped to greet him. He wanted to help Ganesha somehow. Thinking hard on how he could help, he suddenly had a brilliant idea. Narada Muni leaned towards him and whispered in his ear.

'Please go back to Kailash and circumambulate around your respected parents thrice. Your parents are your Universe. You will then win the contest.' Ganesha thanked him profusely and rushed back to Kailash. His parents were surprised to see him back so soon. He then drew a circle around his parents. Then, with folded hands he respectfully walked along the circle three times.

‘I have circled the world thrice because I have learnt from you that your parents are your Universe. Nothing is bigger than them. So I am back after circling my world thrice.’ Parvati hugged Ganesha with love and pride. ‘I declare you the winner of the race,’ said an ecstatic Shiva.

Since then, Ganesha is known as Vighnaharta and is worshipped as the destroyer of all obstacles. He is also known as Vinayaka,Vighnesvara, Ganapathi, and by numerous other names. He is worshipped first and foremost for an auspicious beginning of all new projects and is one of the most loved among Hindu gods.

Hindus across the world celebrate Ganesh Chaturthi in honour of Lord Ganesha, in the month of August or September.